mel bay presents

christmas solos for beginning saxophone

level 1

Online PDF

by mike buerk

To Access the Online Piano Accompaniment Download Go To:
www.melbay.com/94720EB

Contents

Hark, The Herald Angels Sing

Christmas Melodies for Alto Saxophone
E Flat Alto Saxophone Part

O Little Town of Bethlehem

Christmas Melodies for Alto Saxophone
E Flat Alto Saxophone Part

Deck The Halls

Christmas Melodies for Alto Saxophone
E Flat Alto Saxophone Part

Once In Royal David's City

Christmas Melodies for Alto Saxophone
E Flat Alto Saxophone Part

Away In a Manger

Christmas Melodies for Alto Saxophone
E Flat Alto Saxophone Part

The First Noel

Christmas Melodies for Alto Saxophone
E Flat Alto Saxophone Part

Ding Dong, Merrily on High

Christmas Melodies for Alto Saxophone
E Flat Alto Saxophone Part

O Come All Ye Faithful

Christmas Melodies for Alto Saxophone
E Flat Alto Saxophone Part

The Rocking Carol

Christmas Melodies for Alto Saxophone
E Flat Alto Saxophone Part

Joy to The World

Christmas Melodies for Alto Saxophone
E Flat Alto Saxophone Part

15

O Holy Night

Christmas Melodies for Alto Saxophone
Alto Saxophone Part

16

Silent Night

Christmas Melodies for Alto Saxophone
Alto Saxophone Part

Hark, The Herald Angels Sing

Christmas Melodies for Tenor Saxophone
B Flat Tenor Saxophone Part

O Little Town of Bethlehem

Christmas Melodies for Tenor Saxophone
B Flat Tenor Saxophone Part

Deck The Halls

Christmas Melodies for Tenor Saxophone
B Flat Tenor Saxophone Part

Once In Royal David's City

Christmas Melodies for Tenor Saxophone
B Flat Tenor Saxophone Part

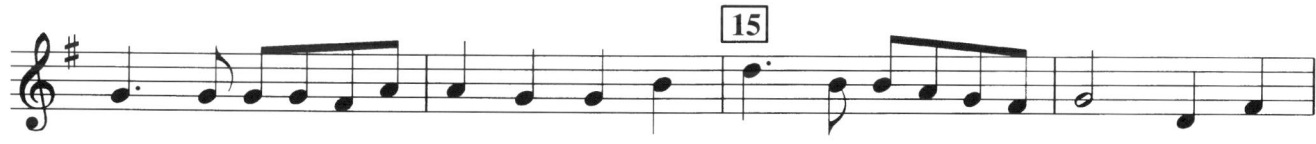

Away in a Manger

Christmas Melodies for Tenor Saxophone
B Flat Tenor Saxophone Part

This page has
been left blank to
avoid awkward
page turns

The First Noel

Christmas Melodies for Tenor Saxophone
B Flat Tenor Saxophone Part

Ding Dong, Merrily on High

Christmas Melodies for Tenor Saxophone
B Flat Tenor Saxophone Part

O Come All Ye Faithful

Christmas Melodies for Tenor Saxophone
B Flat Tenor Saxophone Part

The Rocking Carol

Christmas Melodies for Tenor Saxophone
B Flat Tenor Saxophone Part

28

Joy To The World

Christmas Melodies for Tenor Saxophone
B Flat Tenor Saxophone Part

29

O Holy Night

Christmas Melodies for Tenor Saxophone
B Flat Tenor Saxophone Part

Silent Night

Christmas Melodies for Tenor Saxophone
B Flat Tenor Saxphone Part

PIANO ACCOMPANIMENT

mel bay presents

christmas solos for beginning saxophone

level 1

by mike buerk

1 2 3 4 5 6 7 8 9 0

Contents

Hark, The Herald Angels Sing

Christmas Melodies for Alto Saxophone
Piano Part

4

5

O Little Town of Bethlehem

Christmas Melodies for Alto Saxophone
Piano Part

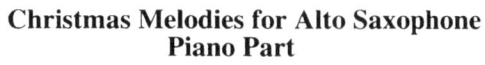

7

Deck The Halls

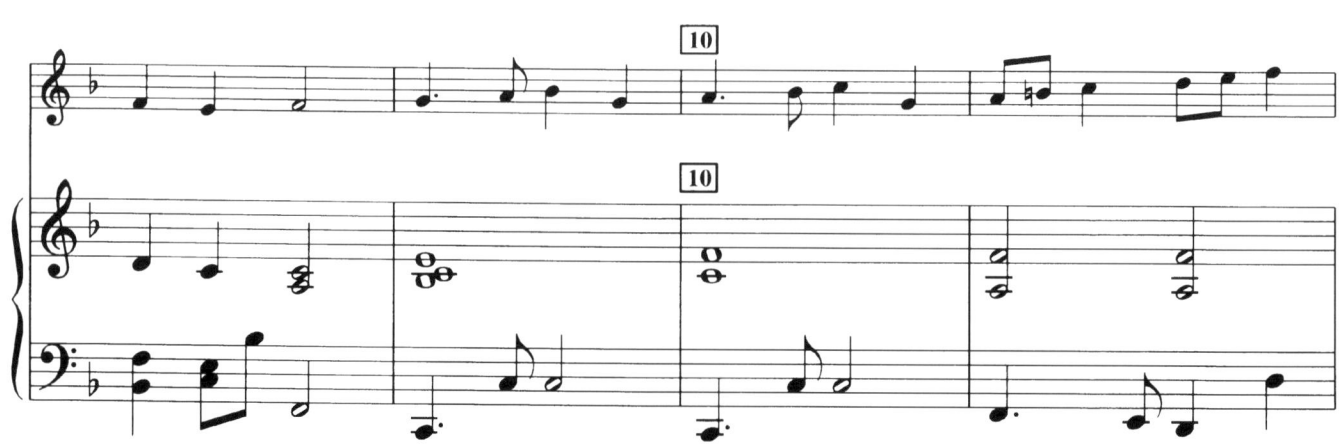

9

This page has
been left blank to
avoid awkward
page turns

Once In Royal David's City

Christmas Solos for Alto Saxophone and Piano

13

Away In a Manger

Christmas Alto Saxophone with Piano

The First Noel

Christmas Melodies for Alto Saxophone
Piano Part

18

19

Ding Dong, Merrily on High

Christmas Melodies for Alto Saxophone

21

O Come All Ye Faithful

Christmas Melodies for Alto Saxophone

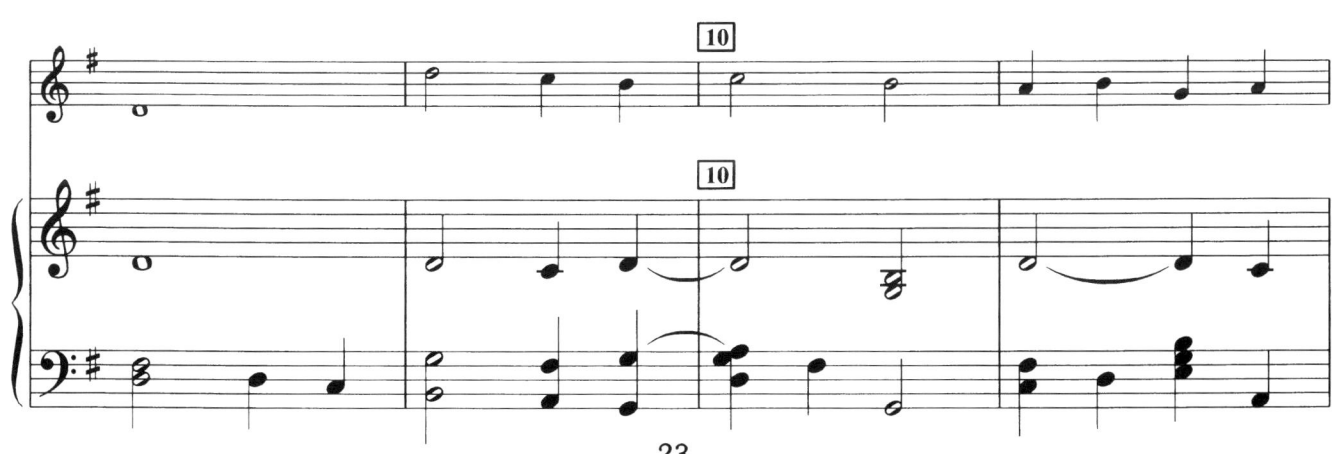

25

The Rocking Carol

Christmas Melodies for Alto Saxophone
Piano Part

27

Joy To The Word

Christmas Melodies for Alto Saxophone
Piano Part

29

O Holy Night

Christmas Melodies for Alto Saxophone
Piano Part

33

Silent Night

Christmas Melodies for Alto Saxophone
Piano Part

36

Made in the USA
San Bernardino, CA
23 November 2015